You

This delightful book is the latest in the series of Ladybird books which have been specially planned to help grown-ups with the world about them.

As in the other books in this series, the large clear script, the careful choice of words, the frequent repetition and the thoughtful matching of text with pictures all enable grown-ups to think they have taught themselves to cope. The subject of the book will greatly appeal to grown-ups.

Series 999

THE LADYBIRD
BOOKS FOR GROWN-UPS SERIES

THE
DO-GOODER

by

J.A. HAZELEY, N.S.F.W. and J.P. MORRIS, O.M.G.

(Authors of 'Eat This Journal!')

Publishers: Ladybird Books Ltd., Loughborough
Printed in England. If wet, Italy.

The do—gooder does all sorts of crazy things.

It can be something as easy as running a marathon, or as difficult as dressing up.

To make this eccentric behaviour seem less like a cry for help or the beginnings of a substantial personal crisis, the do—gooder does it for charity.

For this year's Comic Relief, Ed Sheeran and the man from Poldark are swimming from Land's End to John O'Groats.

David Walliams has already done it twice, so the challenge this year is to do it underwater, while carrying a string bag of eclairs.

People who do not want to run a whole marathon can do a half marathon.

Jellicoe has a fear of heights, so he is doing a half sky-dive.

He will be picked up by a balloon at **1600** feet.

John Bishop was brave enough to tackle a 24-hour screaming challenge for Comic Relief.

Doctors have warned fans that the live DVD will be out in time for Christmas.

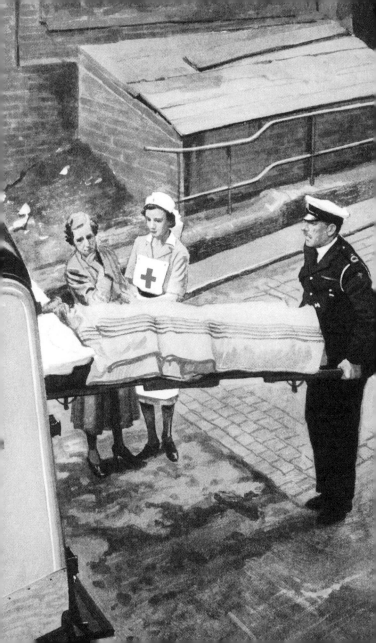

Vernon has a job as a street fundraiser for the R.N.L.I.

He wears a high–visibility jacket, a high–visibility bag and high–visibility trousers.

Everybody on the street still pretends they cannot see him.

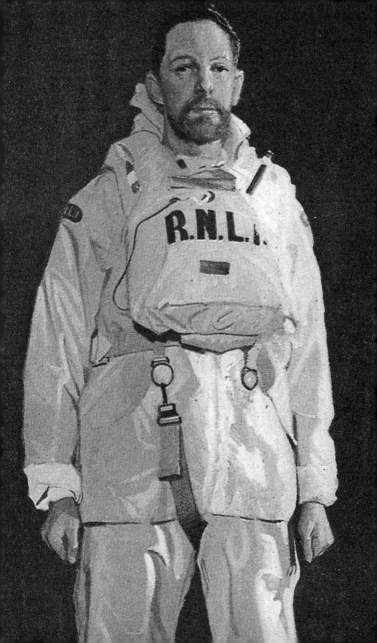

Every penny that Anthony raised for this food run was spent on vital supplies.

He hired the cheapest boat he could find and chose not to waste money on a G.P.S. system, compass, or professional captain.

"I didn't expect Africa to be so cold," says Anthony as he unloads the rice parcels into the snow.

Mr Carisbrooke is growing an amusing Victorian beard in aid of his Gilbert and Sullivan society's "Marchtache" fundraiser.

He has decided he is too busy to ask his employees for sponsorship so he puts them all down for £30 each without telling them.

Since it is staff appraisal week, he is sure none of them will mind.

"Mummy, I need the toilet," says Ella.

"Only another 855 lengths to go," says her mummy.

"But Mummy!" says Ella.

"It's for Save the Children," says Mummy firmly.

Martha bought the cookbook full of celebrities' recipes because it was in aid of a good cause.

She is sure she followed the instructions for Derren Brown's cauliflower cheese to the letter.

And yet, three days later, it is still multiplying.

Judith screamed when she found a crumpled letter at the bottom of a sports bag about the school bake–off tomorrow.

"I'm going to bed," she said.

Esme and Harriet hope that their cheese, honey, toothpaste, sultana and OXO biscuits will be a big hit.

In 1988, Bob Geldof restaged his famous Live Aid concert in space.

Sadly an orbital drum solo from Phil Collins dented the broadcast satellite, so everybody back on earth missed this show—stopping zero—gravity performance by the band Queen.

This painting, by David Bowie, is all that survives.

Ottoline is calling Comic Relief to check where her donation is going.

"Do you have any schemes that address problems in Britain?" she asks.

"Specifically Bracknell? Windsor Drive. Number 46. No. We've got clean water already, but we could do with new decking."

Ottoline believes charity begins at home.

"Like the costume?" asks Sean.

Marvin very nearly has a trouser accident.

The nursery fun run is going to see some record times this year.

Nadaniel has persuaded all the staff at his rooftop narrowboat toastaurant to take part in a Hipster Triathlon in aid of Vinyl For Africa.

After the penny–farthing half–marathon stage, they must take to the pool for the Forbidden Events, such as bombing, petting, and smoking, and lastly run ten miles in Poundstretcher trainers before they become fashionable.

At this Save the Planet concert, singer Gwen Stefani shows she knows how to make a grand entrance.

Her private jet will now crash safely into the sea or an unimportant town.

Tickets to the fundraising dinner cost £200 per head, including the promise of live music.

Gulliver has been playing his "Bee Gees On Broadway" medley for twenty minutes now.

The organisers are thinking of pretending there is a bomb scare.

Muse have agreed to take part in
a televised baking competition to
raise money for charity.

Dominic, the drummer, turns out
to be very good at piping.

And, for once, all of the band
have high hats.

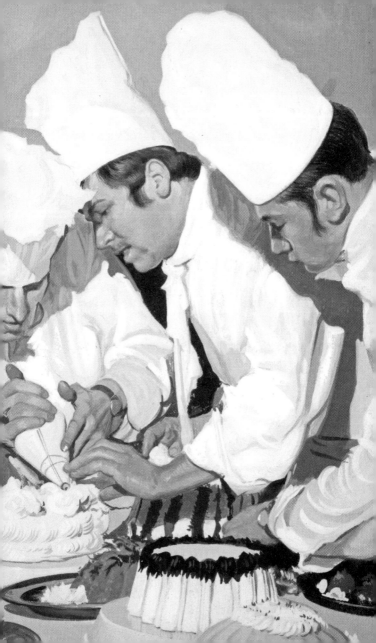

Tansy and Wolfram are collecting the sponsorship money for their playground run.

"£640, please, Mum," says Tansy.

Mum realises she must have written "£20" in the "per lap" box rather than the "total" box again.

Last year the school named a diving board after her.

Sponsored Talk Like A Pirate Day has gone down very badly at The Samaritans.

"Yarr! Have ye tried telling her how ye feels, Jim Lad?" asks Hugo to the sobbing caller.

Helen has set up JustGiving pages for her sponsored breakfasts, sponsored school runs, sponsored commutes, sponsored lunches, sponsored dinners, sponsored sleep, sponsored social media updates, and now sponsored drinking every night for a month in aid of Hungovember.

Her friends are thinking of staging a sponsored intervention.

Bridget has been riding a tortoise from Daventry to Halesowen for Red Nose Day since 2009.

Her schoolwork has suffered but she has raised over £170.

"It's incredible to think that only ten years ago, this place had no running water," says Lenny Henry.

A combination of charity and global warming has changed the village beyond recognition.

Five years ago, Maxton texted the word "GOOSE" to a number on an advert to donate £3 to a goose sanctuary.

He now receives a bi-monthly 80-page goose magazine, weekly goose updates by telephone, and once a year, a birthday card with a goose on it.

Maxton certainly got his money's worth.

"Keep bouncing, Christopher," says Jasmine.

"There's still famine."

THE AUTHORS would like to record their gratitude and offer their apologies to the many Ladybird artists whose luminous work formed the glorious wallpaper of countless childhoods. Revisiting it for this book as grown-ups has been a privilege.

MICHAEL JOSEPH

UK | USA | Canada | Ireland | Australia
India | New Zealand | South Africa

Michael Joseph is part of the Penguin Random House group of companies whose addresses can be found at global.penguinrandomhouse.com

First published 2017
001

Printed in Italy by L.E.G.O. S.p.A

A CIP catalogue record for this book is available from the British Library

ISBN: 978–0–718–18447–6

www.greenpenguin.co.uk

MIX
Paper from
responsible sources
FSC® C018179
www.fsc.org

Penguin Random House is committed to a sustainable future for our business, our readers and our planet. This book is made from Forest Stewardship Council® certified paper.